P9-DNK-275

PRESIDENTS OF THE U.S.A.

# BENJAMIN HARRISON
## OUR TWENTY-THIRD PRESIDENT

*by Sandra Francis*

THE CHILD'S WORLD®

**The Child's World**

Published in the United States of America

The Child's World®
1980 Lookout Drive • Mankato, MN 56003-1705
800-599-READ • www.childsworld.com

Acknowledgments
The Child's World®: Mary Berendes, Publishing Director

The Creative Spark: Mary McGavic, Project Director; Shari Joffe, Editorial Director; Deborah Goodsite, Photo Research; Nancy Ratkiewich, Page Production

The Design Lab: Kathleen Petelinsek, Design

Content Adviser: Phyllis Geeslin, Director, President Benjamin Harrison Home, Indianapolis, Indiana


Photos
Cover and page 3: White House Historical Association (White House Collection) (detail); White House Historical Association (White House Collection)

Interior: Alamy: 13, 29 and 39 (North Wind Picture Archives); The Art Archive: 14 (Private collection Washington/Laurie Platt Winfrey) (detail), 18 (National Portrait Gallery Washington) (detail); Art Resource, NY: 35 (detail) and 39 (National Portrait Gallery, Smithsonian Institution); The Bridgeman Art Library: 23, 26 (Private Collection, Peter Newark American Pictures); Corbis: 11, 19, 32 (Bettmann), 15 and 38, 34 (Corbis); Benjamin Harrison Presidential Site: 4, 8 left and right, 9, 10, 16, 20, 28, 31, 33, 36, 37; The Granger Collection, New York: 5 and 38, 7, 30; The Image Works: 22 (Andre Jenny); iStockphoto: 44 (Tim Fan); Jupiter Images: 27 (Elizabeth Carmel); Library of Congress: 17; North Wind Picture Archives: 24 (North Wind); U.S. Air Force photo: 45.

Library of Congress Cataloging-in-Publication Data
Francis, Sandra.
  Benjamin Harrison / by Sandra Francis.
    p. cm.— (Presidents of the U.S.A.)
  Includes bibliographical references and index.
  ISBN 978-1-60253-052-2 (library bound : alk. paper)
  1. Harrison, Benjamin, 1833–1901—Juvenile literature. 2. Presidents—United States—Biography—Juvenile literature. I. Title. II. Series.

E702.F729 2008
973.8'6'092—dc22
[B]

2007042603

Benjamin Harrison is
the only U.S. president
whose grandfather
was also president.

# TABLE OF CONTENTS

# A FAMILY OF LEADERS

**B**enjamin Harrison, the 23rd president of the United States, came from a long line of famous **politicians.** He was named for his great grand-father, who was a signer of the Declaration of Independence. Benjamin's grandfather, William Henry Harrison, was the first governor of the Indiana **Territory** and the nation's ninth president. Benjamin's father, John Scott Harrison, represented Ohio as a U.S. representative. **Politics** and serving the people became a family tradition.

Benjamin was born on his grandfather's farm in Ohio on August 20, 1833. He was the second of ten children. Soon after Benjamin was born, his grandfather gave his father a piece of land to farm. It was a large, fertile strip located at the place where the Ohio and the Big Miami rivers came together. The family called their farm The Point.

*Benjamin Harrison was the nation's 23rd president. Few other presidents have had such a long family history of government service.*

John Harrison and his wife Elizabeth built a large house at The Point for their growing family. John also built a log schoolhouse. With their own private teachers and their grandfather's vast history library, the Harrison children received a good education.

Religion and family activities were important to the Harrison family. Sundays were spent at church services, which were often followed by family gatherings. Ben and his brothers worked hard on the farm. After growing and harvesting the crops, they hauled them to the river. There they loaded the crops on flatboats and shipped them to New Orleans. Ben was small for his age, but he often took the lead in the hardest work.

*Benjamin Harrison was born at his grandfather's farm in North Bend, Ohio. His grandparents had purchased the land in 1789. At that time, Ohio was still considered the frontier, a wild region beyond settled lands.*

Harrison's grandfather, William Henry, was the last president born before the start of the **American Revolution**.

Whenever there was time, the Harrison children went fishing and swimming in the river. Ben was an excellent fisherman and hunter. He often provided food for his family. He also enjoyed playing rough games. He wanted to prove that he could be just as strong as his larger brothers.

At age 14, Ben enrolled at Farmers' College in Ohio. There he became friends with Caroline Scott, whom he called Carrie. She was the daughter of Dr. John Scott, a former teacher at the school. Ben later decided to finish his studies at Miami University in Oxford, Ohio. That same year, Carrie became a student at Oxford Female College. After a time, they realized that they wanted to spend the rest of their lives together. They were still too young to marry, but they became engaged. Carrie continued her studies in art and music at Oxford. Ben finished his education in law and religion. He graduated with honors from Miami University in 1852.

While home at The Point for a vacation, Ben learned that his father had borrowed money to pay for his schooling. Now Ben's father had to sell some of his land to pay back what he owed. Ben hadn't known how difficult it had been for his father to pay for his schooling. He decided to finish his education by working as an **apprentice** for a lawyer. This meant he would learn by experience while he worked. He studied in a Cincinnati law office, and by the spring of 1854, Ben passed his law exams. He was then qualified to work as a lawyer.

Meanwhile, John Harrison had been elected a representative to the U.S. Congress. He would have to move to Washington, D.C., to take the position. Although he wanted to go very much, John worried about leaving The Point. His wife had died a few years earlier. He still had young children at home with no mother to raise them.

Ben was proud of his father and wanted to find a solution. He and Carrie decided to wed and then live at The Point. They would care for the rest of the

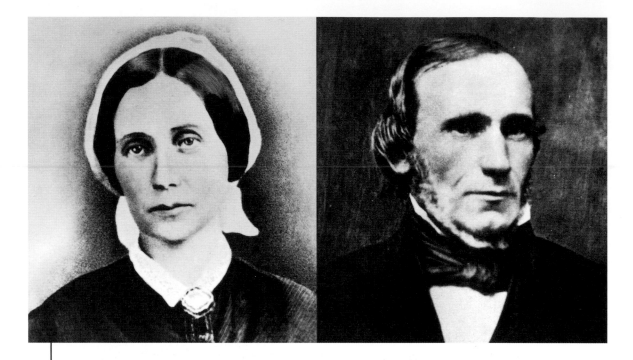

*Harrison's mother, Elizabeth, died while Benjamin was still in his teens. His father, John, took charge of raising their 10 children all by himself.*

family. On October 20, 1853, Carrie and Ben got married. That December, John Harrison accepted his duties in the House of Representatives.

Ben loved living at The Point. But to be successful as a lawyer, he knew he would have to move to a busy city. Later, one of his brothers agreed to return to the farm to live and take over the tasks of caring for the children and the farm. Now Ben and Carrie had to decide where to live. Family and friends encouraged them to settle in Cincinnati. The Harrison family was already well known there, which would help him open a law office. But Ben wanted to be recognized for his own accomplishments, not those of his famous family.

In 1854, he visited Indianapolis, the capital of Indiana. It was growing rapidly, yet still had the feel of a smaller country town. Ben's cousin, William Sheets, lived there. He was a well-known, successful businessman. Having little money, Ben and Carrie gratefully accepted an invitation to live in Sheets's home until they found their own.

When Carrie learned that she was expecting their first child, she returned to Oxford to live with her parents until the baby was born. The Harrisons' first child, Russell Benjamin Harrison, was born on August 12, 1854. Ben worked hard to earn more money. He wanted to bring his wife and child back to a place of their own.

It was difficult to attract clients, but Ben soon had a change of luck. He took a job with the court for $2.50 a day. The pay was small, but it allowed him to meet other lawyers. They began to pay him to help prepare their cases. Soon Ben was well known for his excellent courtroom speeches. By 1855, he was working with another attorney named William Wallace. Together, they built a successful law practice. With Ben's career established, Carrie and Russell returned to Indianapolis. Ben moved his family to a larger, more comfortable house. A second child, Mary (Mamie) Scott Harrison was born on April 3, 1858. Unfortunately, Ben was often too busy to spend much time with his family.

As a young boy, Harrison cut wood and carried water for the family so their cook would have time to fish and hunt with him.

*Carrie Harrison was known for her warmth, wit, and intelligence.*

*Harrison decided to move to Indianapolis to seek his fortune. It took a few years for him to make a name for himself, but he later ran the busy and successful law office shown at right.*

As an adult, Harrison was just five feet, six inches (168 cm) tall. Only one other president was shorter: James Madison. He stood less than five feet, four inches (163 cm) tall.

Ben's interest in politics began during his first year practicing law. He joined the Republican Party and took an active stand against slavery. At age 24, Ben accepted the position of city attorney. In this position, he took charge of legal matters for the city. In 1860, he was elected reporter of the Indiana **Supreme Court.** It was not only an important position, but it paid well, too. The Harrisons were in Indianapolis to stay.

## WILLIAM HENRY HARRISON

Little Benjamin Harrison spent many hours in the **campaign** headquarters of his grandfather, William Henry Harrison. The famous 1840 presidential campaign is said to have been one of the "noisiest, jolliest runs for the office of president in United States history." His grandfather was nicknamed "Old Tippecanoe" because of his victory against Native Americans in the Battle of Tippecanoe in 1811. His running mate for vice president was John Tyler. "Tippecanoe and Tyler, too" became one of the most famous campaign slogans in American history.

William Henry Harrison eventually won the campaign. His **inauguration** took place on March 4, 1841. It was a cold, rainy day. A huge crowd was there to witness the event. In fact, it was the biggest crowd since George Washington had taken the oath of office some 50 years earlier. Even in such bad weather, Harrison gave the longest inaugural speech in history—he spoke for 1 hour and 40 minutes! Later that day, he came down with a bad cold. His illness quickly grew more serious. William Henry Harrison had the misfortune to become the first president to die in office. Just one month after he became president, Harrison died of **pneumonia**. His was the shortest presidency in U.S. history.

# A CALL TO WAR

**D**uring the 1850s, the people of the Northern states became more and more against the practice of slavery. But Southerners refused to give up their slaves. They were sure they could never run their large farms, called plantations, without slaves to plant and harvest their crops. The issue was tearing the nation apart. By the early 1860s, it appeared that the country could not avoid a **civil war.**

In April of 1861, the South fired on Fort Sumter, a U.S. fort in South Carolina. At the time, Benjamin Harrison was busy building a successful law practice. He had joined the Republican Party and served as secretary to the Republican state central committee of Indiana. In 1857, he was elected city attorney. In 1860, he was elected to be reporter of the Supreme Court. He was also well known as an excellent campaign speaker.

With the outbreak of war, however, Benjamin wanted to join the **Union** forces at once. He wanted to fight for his country, just as his famous grandfather had. President Lincoln issued an urgent request for 6,000 volunteer soldiers from Indiana. When 12,000

men signed on, Harrison decided that he should stay with his family and continue practicing law.

By July of 1862, Harrison knew it was time for him to go to war. The conflict between the North and the South continued to rage, but the number of men who were joining the army decreased. The governor of Indiana asked Harrison to **recruit** men into the army. Lieutenant Harrison's first recruit was his law partner and friend, William Wallace. By August 8, Harrison, now a colonel, had recruited 1,000 men. They became known as the 70th Indiana **Regiment.**

Harrison and his troops traveled to Bowling Green, Kentucky, where they guarded the Louisville and Nashville Railroad. It was a rather dull assignment, but it gave them time to train as soldiers prepared to face the enemy. With his own money, Harrison hired

*The Civil War began when the **Confederates**— soldiers from the South—attacked Fort Sumter in 1861.*

In 1864, Colonel Harrison and his troops took part in General William Sherman's march on Atlanta (above).

an expert soldier to coach him so he would become a good military leader. He spent his days learning to give his troops the best possible training. In the evenings, he read books about military **strategy** and wrote letters to Carrie.

The 70th Indiana Regiment guarded the Union railways in Kentucky and Tennessee for nearly two years. Finally, Harrison's strict training paid off in his first real battle. He and his men defeated a band of Confederate soldiers in Kentucky. A surprise attack trapped the enemy troops. Having captured their supplies and horses, the 70th Indiana Regiment returned to their post pleased with their success.

For a time, Harrison and his men saw little action. While they waited for orders, he continued intense training to prepare for battle. This made him unpopular with some soldiers. At last, in January of 1864, Harrison and his men were called to join the troops of generals William Sherman and Ulysses S. Grant. Their goal was to seize Atlanta.

Getting there was not an easy march. The officers in charge had horses to ride, but the other soldiers

Although Harrison showed great bravery during the Civil War, he did worry about losing his life. "I am thinking much of you and the dear children," he once wrote to his wife. "Many earnest prayers will I send up to God this night, should you lose a husband and they a father in this fight."

*Because his grandfather was known as an excellent soldier, Harrison had a lot to live up to during the Civil War. As it turned out, he fought more battles in six months than his grandfather did in his entire life. Harrison became known for his bravery and was promoted to the rank of brigadier general. He is shown here at far left with Union generals Ward, Dustin, and Cogswell.*

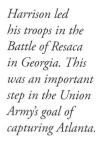

Carrie Harrison visited her husband twice during the war. Her visits convinced Harrison that he needed to devote more time to his family once the war was over.

had to walk. Many of the men became sick and weak. Many times, Colonel Harrison got down from his own horse to let an ill soldier ride. After a battle at New Hope Church, he rolled up his sleeves and cared for the wounded men until the doctors arrived late that night. Even though he could be tough, his kindness and concern made his soldiers respect and admire their leader. They nicknamed him "Little Ben."

Colonel Harrison was not as experienced as other Union leaders, but he led his troops in two great victories. In the first battle, they charged over difficult ground to drive Confederate troops from the town of Resaca. This victory was the first step in capturing Atlanta.

Harrison was called to fight in many more battles. The Confederates decided to attack Sherman's forces in late July of 1864. They hoped to divide the Union

*Harrison led his troops in the Battle of Resaca in Georgia. This was an important step in the Union Army's goal of capturing Atlanta.*

In the capture of Atlanta, Harrison led his troops to two great victories. The most famous was the Battle of Peachtree Creek. When Confederates tried to drive between the Union troops to separate them, Harrison quickly charged his men into battle, shouting, "Come on boys, we're not licked yet!" Running the Confederates out of the area was a major victory for the Union.

troops in half and make them less powerful. Harrison quickly mounted his horse, shouting, "Come on, boys, we're not licked yet!" He then led his men to victory.

After this battle, called the Battle of Peachtree Creek, Harrison was elevated to the rank of brigadier general. He also became known as a hero. By September 1, the Union troops had driven the Confederates out of Atlanta. Afterward, General Sherman gave them a

For years after the war, Harrison attended many Civil War reunions to meet with other former soldiers.

*Harrison supported the reelection of Abraham Lincoln (above), who had led the nation with strength during the Civil War.*

well-deserved rest. Indiana's governor requested that Harrison be sent to Indianapolis for special duty. The assignment gave him a short reunion with his family.

While Harrison was away, another man had taken over his position as reporter of the Supreme Court. The governor wanted Harrison to campaign to win his job back. He also asked him to recruit more Indiana men for the Union army. News of Harrison's heroism in Georgia had spread throughout Indiana, so it was easy for him to recruit men. He also campaigned for President Abraham Lincoln, who was running for a second **term** as president. Both Harrison and Lincoln won in the November elections.

In December of 1864, Harrison and his men returned to duty. Their job was to drive Confederate General John Hood out of Tennessee. Their victory ended the war in that state. For his efforts, Harrison received a second leave of duty, which allowed him to return home for a brief time.

After a short visit, Harrison went to South Carolina, where he trained replacement troops for a few months. In April, he planned to rejoin his regiment in North Carolina. On the way, he learned that Confederate General Robert E. Lee's army had **surrendered.** Soon the war was over, and the Union was saved. Huge celebrations took place for days. But then tragedy struck the nation. Just six days later, on April 14, 1865, President Lincoln was **assassinated.**

Harrison arrived in North Carolina on the same day that news of the tragedy reached the people. The streets were empty, for the South had been **devastated** by the war. In the Union camps, flags hung sadly at half-mast in honor of President Lincoln. When Harrison learned that Lincoln was dead, he was shocked and full of grief. By request, he delivered a speech at a memorial service honoring the president.

On May 24, 1865, a parade took place in Washington, D.C., to celebrate the end of the war and to honor the troops who saved the Union. Harrison and the 70th Indiana Regiment fell in line and proudly marched as heroes behind General Sherman. But before they did, Harrison gave a speech to his men. With great sincerity, he said, "The highest honors are due to the men who bore the cartridge and the gun. What were your officers without you?"

When Harrison became president, he worked to make sure that men who had fought in the Civil War received government **pensions**, or money to reward them for their service.

*The happy events celebrating the Union's victory came to an abrupt end when President Lincoln was assassinated. During Lincoln's funeral procession, thousands of people lined the streets to show their respect for the great leader.*

# CAROLINE SCOTT HARRISON

Caroline Lavinia Scott was born in Oxford, Ohio, on October 1, 1832. Her father, a Presbyterian minister and teacher, owned and ran a school for girls in Oxford. As a young woman, Carrie attended classes there. Young Benjamin Harrison was enrolled at nearby Miami University. It was there that Benjamin and Carrie fell in love and became secretly engaged.

After marrying Benjamin, Carrie helped him care for his younger brothers and sisters while their father was in Washington. She was a devoted mother to their children, Russell and Mamie, and a great help to Benjamin as he worked long hours to establish his career. In 1861 they had another daughter who died at birth.

Carrie was known for her lively spirit and intelligence. Her artistic ability and musical talent helped to make the White House a better place to live for her family. When Benjamin was elected president, Carrie insisted that the White House receive much-needed repairs. It had become very run-down over the years. She supervised the renovations right down to the last detail. Electricity was installed in the White House for the first time. Carrie Harrison believed that everything in the White House should be special. She went into the White House basement and identified pieces of china used by previous administrations, then put it on display for the public. She even designed a new pattern of china for the White House.

Carrie presided as first lady in the White House during the U.S. Centennial celebration of 1889. As part of the celebration, she helped found an organization called Daughters of the American Revolution (DAR). She also served as the first president-general of the DAR. Carrie's interest in women's rights prompted her to help collect funds to establish the Johns Hopkins Medical School. The funds were granted on the condition that women would be admitted, too.

Carrie died in the White House in October of 1892. Benjamin had refused to campaign for a second term while she was so ill and stayed by her side to the end. Caroline Scott Harrison is buried in the Crown Hill Cemetery in Indianapolis.

# A WORTHY CANDIDATE

The years Benjamin had spent away from home took a toll on his marriage and family life. After he left the 70th Regiment on June 8, 1865, he vowed to spend more time with his family. Russell was now ten years old, and Mamie was seven. Benjamin felt that he hardly knew them. Together they enjoyed going for rides in their horse-drawn buggy and visiting with friends at church dinners. Benjamin and Russell spent more time fishing and hunting together. He even took Mrs. Harrison to the theater and opera. But it was not long before Benjamin was working too hard again. He gained weight and often complained of not feeling well.

By April of 1867, he became so exhausted that he couldn't work for several weeks. Something had to change, so he decided to give up the tiring position of reporter. After a relaxing fishing trip in Minnesota, Harrison was ready to return to his law practice. But he also hoped one day to continue his career in politics.

Harrison was a member of the Republican Party, one of the two major U.S. **political parties.** In 1876, the Republican Party asked him to be their **candidate**

for governor of Indiana after their first choice withdrew because of a scandal. Harrison agreed to run, but ended up losing the election. Still, the campaign brought him to the attention of Indiana's citizens.

Except for the death of Harrison's father, the 1870s were good years for the family. In 1875, they built a lovely home in Indianapolis. Mrs. Harrison planted gardens and enjoyed taking care of them. Mamie grew into a pretty and popular young woman. Russell graduated from Lafayette College.

*In the 1870s, the Harrison family lived in this home in Indianapolis, Indiana.*

*The Republicans chose James Garfield and Chester A. Arthur as their presidential and vice-presidential candidates in the 1880 election. Benjamin Harrison, a Republican, traveled around campaigning for them.*

In 1880, Indiana Republicans sent Harrison to the Republican National Convention in Chicago. The purpose of this large meeting was to select the Republican candidate for the next presidential election. Several men were being considered, but no one was the favorite. The men at the convention voted 33 times before they came to a decision. At last, they selected James A. Garfield of Ohio. Throughout Garfield's campaign, Harrison traveled around Indiana and other states, giving speeches that helped the Republicans win the presidency. Benjamin Harrison became known and respected throughout the nation.

In 1881, Harrison was elected to the U.S. Senate. President Garfield offered him a position in his **cabinet,** but Harrison refused it. He believed that his abilities would be more valuable in the Senate. He also thought it was a better place to further his own goals in politics. For one thing, Harrison felt he could

The Republican Party first considered **nominating** Harrison as their presidential candidate in 1884, but he did not run for the office until four years later.

23

meet other important leaders who might offer him their support in future elections.

The Harrisons moved to Washington, where they would live for the next six years. But in their first year there, tragedy struck the nation again. President Garfield was assassinated, and Vice President Chester A. Arthur became president.

Harrison did not have a good relationship with Arthur. When it was time to select a candidate for the next presidential election, Harrison campaigned for James G. Blaine of Maine. Blaine was chosen as the Republican candidate, but he did not win the presidency. Grover Cleveland, who belonged to the Democratic Party, won the election.

Six years in the Senate taught Harrison how the United States political system worked. His career was enjoyable, except for the daily stream of people who came to him asking for jobs or favors. Harrison did not believe in giving jobs to people who were not qualified to do the work. He always agreed to meet with **veterans** of the army, however. He supported these men until the end of his life. Harrison was known as someone who would help those who had once fought for their country. As a member of the Committee on Military Affairs, he supported efforts aimed at building a stronger, more modern navy.

Senator Harrison also helped pass a **bill** that created a new government in the territory of Alaska. Before that time, the military had controlled Alaska. Now the people who lived there could take control of their government. Harrison wanted many of the territories in the West to become states. He helped lay the groundwork for this to take place in future years. He also tried to protect a beautiful site on the Colorado River known as the Grand Canyon. Harrison was the first senator to suggest making this area a national park.

Harrison accomplished much during his six years in the Senate. But while he was away, members of the Democratic Party replaced the Republicans in Indiana's state government. In 1887, Harrison was not reelected to the Senate. He was sorry to lose his position, but he was now free to pursue his greatest career goal—the presidency. In 1888, he became a candidate for that office.

*Harrison appears as a champion of American industry in this campaign poster. His support during the election came largely from businessmen who agreed with Harrison's call for a high protective tariff. A tariff is a tax on foreign goods. Businessmen supported a high tariff because it encouraged Americans to buy products made in the United States.*

## THE GRAND CANYON

Senator Harrison admired Arizona's Grand Canyon and believed the U.S. government should protect this natural wonder. He wanted Congress to create a national park in the region. The national parks are public grounds set aside for people to visit and enjoy. They preserve wilderness and honor important events in history. Yellowstone, located in Wyoming and Montana, was the first national park, created in 1872.

Senator Harrison introduced bills in 1882, 1883, and again in 1886 to establish Grand Canyon National Park. His fellow lawmakers refused to pass them. Although Harrison was not able to reach this goal while he was in the Senate, his efforts eventually paid off. As president, Harrison created the Grand Canyon Forest Reserve, a first step toward his goal. Finally, in 1918, Congress passed a bill establishing the Grand Canyon National Park. President Woodrow Wilson signed it into law on February 26, 1919.

# CHAPTER FOUR

# THE CENTENNIAL PRESIDENT

**A**fter a colorful campaign, Benjamin Harrison was elected president of the United States. His 1889 inauguration took place 100 years after George Washington took office, so Harrison became known as the "Centennial President." A centennial is a 100th anniversary.

Harrison won the election, but it was a very close vote. He received 100,000 fewer votes from the American people than President Grover Cleveland did. But he won 233 **electoral votes,** while Cleveland won only 168. Although many Americans wanted Cleveland to stay in office, Harrison became the new leader.

*An 1888 campaign button in support of Benjamin Harrison.*

The people of Indiana were proud of him. As he prepared to leave for Washington, they gave him a grand send-off.

On a cold and rainy day in the nation's capital, Benjamin Harrison became the 23rd president of the United States. His first job was to choose a cabinet.

President Harrison selected men with experience. Whenever he had to make important decisions such as this, he refused to let others tell him what to do. This angered many important Republicans. They wanted him to take their advice. As a result, Harrison lost their support.

Harrison had many goals he hoped to achieve. He was one of the first presidents to succeed in foreign affairs, which are matters involving other countries. His work brought about better relations with other nations. He wanted to build friendships with other

Benjamin Harrison was the first president to have a decorated Christmas tree in the White House.

*Harrison's inauguration took place on March 4, 1889, a rainy and cold day. Even in such bad weather, a huge crowd gathered for the event. Grover Cleveland, the outgoing president, held an umbrella over Harrison's head as he took the oath of office.*

*Harrison (center) posed for this portrait with his cabinet. When he became president, many people asked him for positions in government. Harrison said that filling the positions was a "frightful ordeal." Most people who asked for jobs were "worthy men and many of them are personal friends." But he could not aid every person who sought his help.*

countries on the American continents. To achieve this, the first Pan-American Congress met in Washington, D.C., in 1889. Representatives from many countries attended the meeting.

President Harrison led the way for six territories to enter the Union. The Omnibus Bill of 1889 allowed North Dakota, South Dakota, Montana, and Washington to become states. Wyoming and Idaho became states in 1890. Harrison also asked the Senate to make Hawaii a U.S. territory. Unfortunately, the next president stopped this from happening when he took office. Harrison was greatly disappointed by this.

*The White House was in a terrible state when Harrison became president. In fact, there was talk of replacing it with a new mansion for the president. Finally, the government decided to repair the historic home. This photograph shows the redecorated East Room of the White House during Harrison's presidency.*

When there was talk of building a new president's mansion, Mrs. Harrison threw herself into the project with enthusiasm. Then the government decided to repair the White House instead. She led the efforts to refurbish it, using $35,000 that the government had set aside for the project.

Harrison and many congressmen also wanted to pass the Force Bill. It would have provided government protection to black voters during elections in the South. After the Civil War, white people often threatened blacks who tried to vote. They even created state laws to stop them from voting. The House of Representatives passed the Force Bill. Unfortunately, the Senate refused to pass it, so it did not become a law.

One victory during Harrison's term was the Dependent Pension Act, passed in 1890. It granted

President and Mrs. Harrison were the first residents of the White House to have electricity.

money to veterans who had been permanently injured in battle. Harrison and his advisors also continued a huge shipbuilding program. This helped build superior naval forces for the United States.

One of the most important achievements during Harrison's time in office was the Sherman Antitrust Act of 1890. This law allowed the government to make sure companies ran their businesses fairly. It stopped the most powerful companies in the nation from creating **trusts,** which are partnerships between large companies that are formed to put smaller ones out of business. Harrison and members of Congress wanted to help all American businesses succeed. Another way to accomplish this was the McKinley Tariff. A tariff is a tax on foreign goods to make them cost more. Congress hoped the McKinley Tariff would make Americans buy more products made in the United States. Unfortunately, many people did not like the tariff and the higher prices it created. It made Harrison and many Republicans in Congress unpopular with the people and hurt their chances for reelection.

Even though he had lost a lot of support from the Republican Party, Harrison was nominated to run for a second term. Mrs. Harrison became very ill during this time. When the president learned that she did not have long to live, he refused to leave her side to

*Harrison's grandson, also named Benjamin, lived at the White House with his family during the early 1890s. Little Benjamin was often photographed as he drove his goat cart around the grounds. The goat once ran away with the boy and raced down the White House driveway onto Pennsylvania Avenue. The president himself, dressed in a top hat and long black coat, ran after them in hot pursuit.*

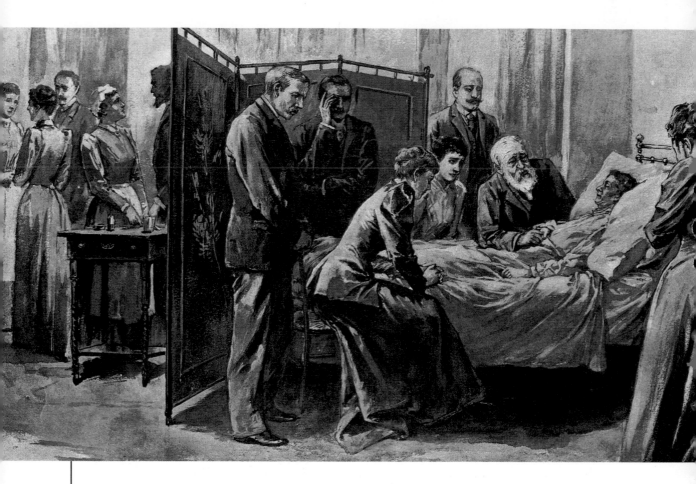

*In the summer of 1891, Carrie Harrison developed a bad cough. She became much weaker the following year. Soon she could not leave her bed. Doctors said she had tuberculosis, a serious disease that affects the lungs. Unfortunately, she never recovered. She died at the White House on October 25, 1892.*

campaign for office. On October 25, 1892, his beloved Carrie died at the White House.

Most Americans wanted to elect a Democrat as the next president. Grover Cleveland won the election. He became the only president ever to be reelected after having been voted out of office. When Harrison received the news that he had lost the election, he was too sad about Mrs. Harrison's death to care. "Political defeat carries no personal grief," he said. After Cleveland's inauguration, Harrison returned to Indianapolis. He continued to work as a lawyer and spent many hours writing articles for magazines and newspapers. He also wrote a book titled *This Country of Ours.*

After being alone for three years, Harrison married a young widow, Mary Lord Dimmick, who was Carrie's niece. Soon they had a child, whom they named Elizabeth. The marriage and new baby gave Harrison great joy. His Republican friends hinted that he should run for president again. Harrison was not interested. He said a new "pilot could steer the Ship of State more satisfactorily."

Harrison continued working until his death from pneumonia on March 13, 1901. His wife and many friends were at his bedside. His body was placed in the Indiana State House, where the survivors of the 70th Indiana Regiment led soldiers and citizens in a parade to honor him.

Many people expressed their admiration for Harrison. They also expressed their sorrow for his death. Former president Grover Cleveland perhaps best described the excellence of Harrison's life when he said, "In public office he was guided by patriotism and devotion to duty— often at the sacrifice of temporary popularity—and in private [life] his influence and example were always in the direction of decency and good citizenship."

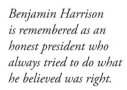

*Benjamin Harrison is remembered as an honest president who always tried to do what he believed was right.*

## FOUR GENERATIONS

Four generations lived in the White House during President Harrison's term. The oldest was 90-year-old Dr. John Scott, Carrie Harrison's father. Mamie came with her two children, Benjamin Harrison McKee and Mary Lodge McKee. Mamie helped her mother with the huge task of entertaining visitors to the White House. Mamie's husband, J. R., traveled between his business in Indianapolis and his family in the White House.

The president's son, Russell, traveled between Washington, D.C., and his ranch and newspaper business in Montana. His wife, Mary, and daughter, Marthena, lived with the rest of the Harrisons at the White House. Mary helped Carrie Harrison manage the household staff. Mrs. Harrison's widowed niece, Mary Lord Dimmick, also lived there. She helped with the chore of writing letters. In this photograph, Mrs. Harrison is holding little Benjamin McKee, Mamie stands in the center, and Dr. Scott is holding Mary.

## MARY DIMMICK HARRISON, HARRISON'S SECOND WIFE

Mary Scott Lord was born in 1858 to Russell and Elizabeth Scott Lord. She was the niece of Caroline Scott Harrison. Mary was educated in the best private school in Princeton, New Jersey, and later attended Elmira College in New York. Her first husband, Walter Dimmick, died six weeks after their marriage, making her a very young widow. Mary often visited her aunt in the White House. Finally, Carrie convinced Mary to live in the White House full time with the Harrison family. Mary assisted Carrie with the children and helped Carrie with letter writing.

Three years after Caroline's death, Mary Dimmick married Benjamin Harrison. She traveled with him to Venezuela to settle a boundary dispute and then to the Hague Peace Conference. Mary and Benjamin had one daughter, Elizabeth, who later became a lawyer in both Indiana and New York.

After Benjamin's death, Mary Harrison moved to New York with her daughter. She was in charge of the entertainment for the Officers Service Department of the New York War Camp Community Service. Mary served as treasurer of the Committee of One Hundred, a Republican Woman's organization, for 25 years. Mary Lord Dimmick Harrison lived in New York City until her death in 1948.

# T I M E   L I N E

| 1830 | 1840 | 1850 | 1860 |
|---|---|---|---|

**1830**
Benjamin Harrison is born on August 20 on the farm of his grandfather, William Henry Harrison. Benjamin is the second of 10 children born to John and Elizabeth Harrison.

**1847**
At age 14, Harrison enters Farmers' College near Cincinnati.

**1851**
Harrison transfers to Miami University in Oxford, Ohio, to finish his education.

**1852**
Harrison graduates from Miami University.

**1853**
Harrison's father, John, is elected to Congress and must move to Washington, D.C. Benjamin Harrison and Caroline Scott marry and move to The Point (Harrison's childhood home). They care for Harrison's younger brothers and sisters who still live at home. Harrison travels to Cincinnati each day to study law.

**1854**
Harrison passes his law exams and visits Indianapolis. He decides to start his law career there. He and his wife move to Indianapolis. Their son, Russell, is born.

**1855**
Harrison forms a law partnership with William Wallace.

**1857**
Harrison becomes the city attorney of Indianapolis.

**1858**
The Harrisons' daughter, Mary (Mamie) Scott, is born.

**1860**
Harrison is elected reporter of the Indiana Supreme Court.

**1861**
The Civil War begins when the South fires on Fort Sumter.

**1862**
Harrison joins the army and becomes a lieutenant. He recruits men for the 70th Indiana Regiment, and his troops are sent to Kentucky and Tennessee to protect railroads for the next two years.

**1864**
Colonel Harrison and his men join Generals Sherman and Grant to capture Atlanta. Harrison leads his men to important victories at the Battles of Resaca and Peachtree Creek. He earns a promotion to brigadier general. In November, Harrison is reelected as reporter of the Indiana Supreme Court.

**1865**
The Confederates surrender, and the Civil War ends. On April 14, President Lincoln is assassinated.

38

| **1870** | **1880** | | **1890** | **1900** |

**1875**
Harrison and Carrie build a home in Indianapolis. It remains the family home until Harrison's death.

**1876**
Harrison wins the nomination for governor of Indiana, but he loses the election.

**1880**
Harrison attends the Republican National Convention in Chicago to select a presidential candidate.

**1881**
1881 Harrison is elected to the U.S. Senate. President Garfield offers him a position in his cabinet, but Harrison refuses it. Later in the year, Garfield is assassinated.

**1882**
Senator Benjamin Harrison introduces the first bill to create Grand Canyon National Park. Congress does not pass it.

**1887**
Harrison is not reelected to the U.S. Senate.

**1888**
Harrison is elected the 23rd president of the United States.

**1889**
Harrison is inaugurated on March 4. The first Pan-American Congress meets in Washington. The Omnibus Bill allows North Dakota, South Dakota, Montana, and Washington to become states.

**1890**
The House passes the Force Bill to protect African American voters in the South; however, the Senate refuses to pass it. The Dependent Pension Act is passed to give money to veterans injured in war. The Sherman Antitrust Act prevents big businesses from creating trusts. The McKinley Tariff is enacted to make Americans buy more products made in the United States. Wyoming and Idaho are admitted to the Union.

**1892**
The Republican Party nominates Harrison to run for a second term. Carrie Harrison dies shortly before the presidential election. Harrison loses the election to Grover Cleveland.

**1893**
President Harrison creates the Grand Canyon Forest Reserve before leaving office.

**1895**
Harrison marries Mary Lord Dimmick.

**1896**
The Harrisons' daughter, Elizabeth, is born.

**1901**
Benjamin Harrison dies on March 13. The survivors of the 70th Indiana Regiment lead soldiers in a parade to honor their leader.

**1948**
Mary Lord Harrison dies.

# GLOSSARY

**American Revolution (uh-MAYR-uh-kuhn rev-uh-LOO-shun)** A revolution is something (such as a war) that causes a complete change in government. During the American Revolution, American colonists fought a war to gain independence from England.

**apprentice (uh-PREN-tis)** An apprentice promises to work for a skilled worker in exchange for learning a business. Harrison decided to study law as an apprentice to a lawyer.

**assassinated (uh-SASS-uh-nay-ted)** Assassinated means murdered, especially a well-known person. President Abraham Lincoln was assassinated on April 14, 1865.

**bill (BILL)** A bill is an idea for a new law that is presented to a group of lawmakers. Harrison helped pass a bill that created a new government in Alaska.

**cabinet (KAB-eh-net)** A cabinet is the group of people who advise a president. President Garfield offered Harrison a post in his cabinet.

**campaign (kam-PAYN)** A campaign is the process of running for an election, including activities such as giving speeches or attending rallies. Harrison was fascinated by his grandfather's campaign for the presidency.

**candidate (KAN-dih-det)** A candidate is a person running for office. In 1872, Harrison hoped to be the Republican candidate for governor of Indiana.

**civil war (SIV-il WAR)** A civil war is a war between opposing groups of citizens within the same country. The American Civil War began in 1861.

**Confederates (kun-FED-ur-uts)** Confederates were people who supported the slave states (or the people who lived in those states) that left the Union in 1861. The people of the South were called Confederates.

**devastated (DEV-uh-stay-ted)** Devastated means brought to ruin by violent action. The South was devastated after the Civil War.

**electoral votes (ee-LEKT-uh-rul VOHTS)** Electoral votes are votes cast by representatives of the American public. Each state chooses representatives who vote for a candidate in a presidential election. These representatives are supposed to vote according to what most people in their state want.

**inauguration (ih-nawg-yuh-RAY-shun)** An inauguration is the ceremony that takes place when a new president begins a term. Harrison's inauguration took place on March 4, 1889.

**monopolize (muh-NOP-uh-lize)** Monopolize means to take complete control over something, such as a service or the supply of a product. In the late 1800s, big trusts tried to monopolize many major businesses.

**nominating (NOM-ih-nayt-ing)** When a political party is nominating someone, it is choosing that person to be its candidate for a political office. The Republican Party considered nominating Harrison as its candidate in 1884.

**pensions (PEN-shuhnz)** Pensions are amounts of money paid regularly to someone who has retired from work. Harrison made sure that men who had fought in the Civil War received government pensions to reward them for their service.

**pneumonia (noo-MOH-nyuh)** Pneumonia is a disease that causes swelling of the lungs, high fever, and difficulty breathing. Harrison died of pneumonia.

**political parties (puh-LIT-uh-kul PAR-teez)** Political parties are groups of people who share similar ideas about how to run a government. Harrison belonged to the Republican political party.

**politicians (pawl-uh-TISH-uhns)** Politicians are people who run for or hold a government office. Harrison came from a family of politicians.

**politics (PAWL-uh-tiks)** Politics refers to the actions and practices of the government. Serving in politics was a tradition in the Harrison family.

**recruit (ree-KREWT)** If people recruit others to a group, they encourage them to join it. The governor of Indiana asked Harrison to recruit men into the army.

**regiment (REJ-eh-ment)** A regiment is a group of soldiers led by a colonel. During the Civil War, Harrison commanded the 70th Indiana Regiment.

**strategy (STRAT-eh-jee)** Strategy is skillful planning to achieve a goal. Harrison read books about military strategy to become a better leader.

**supreme court (suh-PREEM KORT)** A supreme court is the most powerful court in an individual state. Harrison was elected reporter for the Indiana Supreme Court.

**surrendered (suh-REN-durd)** If an army surrendered, it gave up to its enemy. The Confederates surrendered in 1865, ending the Civil War.

**tariff (TAYR-iff)** A tariff is a tax on foreign goods. During his campaign for the presidency, Harrison supported a high protective tariff.

**term (TERM )** A term is the length of time a politician can keep his or her position by law. A U.S. president's term of office is four years.

**territory (TAYR-ih-tor-ee)** A territory is a land or region, especially land that belongs to a government. Harrison encouraged the government to grant statehood to territories.

**trusts (TRUSTS)** Trusts are two or more companies that agree to work together. Trusts try to put other companies out of business to get more business for themselves.

**union (YOON-yen)** A union is the joining together of two people or groups of people, such as states. The Union is another name for the United States.

**veterans (VET-ur-enz)** Veterans are people who have served in the armed forces. Harrison worked to help veterans.

# THE UNITED STATES GOVERNMENT

The United States government is divided into three equal branches: the executive, the legislative, and the judicial. This division helps prevent abuses of power because each branch has to answer to the other two. No one branch can become too powerful.

## EXECUTIVE BRANCH

President
Vice President
Departments

The job of the executive branch is to enforce the laws. It is headed by the president, who serves as the spokesperson for the United States around the world. The president signs bills into law and appoints important officials such as federal judges. He or she is also the commander in chief of the U.S. military. The president is assisted by the vice president, who takes over if the president dies or cannot carry out the duties of the office.

The executive branch also includes various departments, each focused on a specific topic. They include the Defense Department, the Justice Department, and the Agriculture Department. The department heads, along with other officials such as the vice president, serve as the president's closest advisers, called the cabinet.

## LEGISLATIVE BRANCH

Congress
*Senate and
House of Representatives*

The job of the legislative branch is to make the laws. It consists of Congress, which is divided into two parts: the Senate and the House of Representatives. The Senate has 100 members, and the House of Representatives has 435 members. Each state has two senators. The number of representatives a state has varies depending on the state's population.

Besides making laws, Congress also passes budgets and enacts taxes. In addition, it is responsible for declaring war, maintaining the military, and regulating trade with other countries.

## JUDICIAL BRANCH

Supreme Court
Courts of Appeals
District Courts

The job of the judicial branch is to interpret the laws. It consists of the nation's federal courts. Trials are held in district courts. During trials, judges must decide what laws mean and how they apply. Courts of appeals review the decisions made in district courts.

The nation's highest court is the Supreme Court. If someone disagrees with a court of appeals ruling, he or she can ask the Supreme Court to review it. The Supreme Court may refuse. The Supreme Court makes sure that decisions and laws do not violate the Constitution.

# CHOOSING
# THE PRESIDENT

It may seem odd, but American voters don't elect the president directly. Instead, the president is chosen using what is called the Electoral College.

Each state gets as many votes in the Electoral College as its combined total of senators and representatives in Congress. For example, Iowa has two senators and five representatives, so it gets seven electoral votes. Although the District of Columbia does not have any voting members in Congress, it gets three electoral votes. Usually, the candidate who wins the most votes in any given state receives all of that state's electoral votes.

To become president, a candidate must get more than half of the Electoral College votes. There are a total of 538 votes in the Electoral College, so a candidate needs 270 votes to win. If nobody receives 270 Electoral College votes, the House of Representatives chooses the president.

With the Electoral College system, the person who receives the most votes nationwide does not always receive the most electoral votes. This happened most recently in 2000, when Al Gore received half a million more national votes than George W. Bush. Bush became president because he had more Electoral College votes.

# THE WHITE HOUSE

The White House is the official home of the president of the United States. It is located at 1600 Pennsylvania Avenue NW in Washington, D.C. In 1792, a contest was held to select the architect who would design the president's home. James Hoban won. Construction took eight years.

The first president, George Washington, never lived in the White House. The second president, John Adams, moved into the house in 1800, though the inside was not yet complete. During the War of 1812, British soldiers burned down much of the White House. It was rebuilt several years later.

The White House was changed through the years. Porches were added, and President Theodore Roosevelt added the West Wing. President William Taft changed the shape of the presidential office, making it into the famous Oval Office. While Harry Truman was president, the old house was discovered to be structurally weak. All the walls were reinforced with steel, and the rooms were rebuilt.

Today, the White House has 132 rooms (including 35 bathrooms), 28 fireplaces, and 3 elevators. It takes 570 gallons of paint to cover the outside of the six-story building. The White House provides the president with many ways to relax. It includes a putting green, a jogging track, a swimming pool, a tennis court, and beautifully landscaped gardens. The White House also has a movie theater, a billiard room, and a one-lane bowling alley.

# PRESIDENTIAL PERKS

The job of president of the United States is challenging. It is probably one of the most stressful jobs in the world. Because of this, presidents are paid well, though not nearly as well as the leaders of large corporations. In 2007, the president earned $400,000 a year. Presidents also receive extra benefits that make the demanding job a little more appealing.

★ **Camp David:** In the 1940s, President Franklin D. Roosevelt chose this heavily wooded spot in the mountains of Maryland to be the presidential retreat, where presidents can relax. Even though it is a retreat, world business is conducted there. Most famously, President Jimmy Carter met with Middle Eastern leaders at Camp David in 1978. The result was a peace agreement between Israel and Egypt.

★ *Air Force One:* The president flies on a jet called *Air Force One*. It is a Boeing 747-200B that has been modified to meet the president's needs.

*Air Force One* is the size of a large home. It is equipped with a dining room, sleeping quarters, a conference room, and office space. It also has two kitchens that can provide food for up to 50 people.

★ **The Secret Service:** While not the most glamorous of the president's perks, the Secret Service is one of the most important. The Secret Service is a group of highly trained agents who protect the president and the president's family.

★ **The Presidential State Car:** The presidential limousine is a stretch Cadillac DTS.

It has been armored to protect the president in case of attack. Inside the plush car are a foldaway desk, an entertainment center, and a communications console.

★ **The Food:** The White House has five chefs who will make any food the president wants. The White House also has an extensive wine collection.

★ **Retirement:** A former president receives a pension, or retirement pay, of just under $180,000 a year. Former presidents also receive Secret Service protection for the rest of their lives.

# FACTS

## QUALIFICATIONS

To run for president, a candidate must

* be at least 35 years old
* be a citizen who was born in the United States
* have lived in the United States for 14 years

## TERM OF OFFICE

A president's term of office is four years.
No president can stay in office for more than two terms.

## ELECTION DATE

The presidential election takes place every four years on the first Tuesday of November.

## INAUGURATION DATE

Presidents are inaugurated on January 20.

## OATH OF OFFICE

I do solemnly swear I will faithfully execute the office of the President of the United States and will to the best of my ability preserve, protect, and defend the Constitution of the United States.

## WRITE A LETTER TO THE PRESIDENT

One of the best things about being a U.S. citizen is that Americans get to participate in their government. They can speak out if they feel government leaders aren't doing their jobs. They can also praise leaders who are going the extra mile. Do you have something you'd like the president to do? Should the president worry more about the environment and encourage people to recycle? Should the government spend more money on our schools? You can write a letter to the president to say how you feel!

1600 Pennsylvania Avenue
Washington, D.C. 20500
You can even send an e-mail to: president@whitehouse.gov

## BOOKS

Adelson, Bruce. *Benjamin Harrison.* Minneapolis: Twenty-First Century Books, 2007.

Doak, Robin S. *William Henry Harrison.* Minneapolis: Compass Point Books, 2004.

Graham, Martin F., Richard A. Sauers, and George Skoch. *The Blue and the Gray.* Lincolnwood, IL: Publications International, 1996.

Rubel, David. *Scholastic Encyclopedia of the Presidents and Their Times.* New York: Scholastic, 1994.

Williams, Jean Kinney. *Benjamin Harrison: America's 23rd President.* New York: Children's Press, 2004.

## VIDEOS

*The American President.* DVD, VHS (Alexandria, VA: PBS Home Video, 2000).

*The History Channel Presents The Presidents.* DVD (New York: A & E Home Video, 2005).

*National Geographic's Inside the White House.* DVD (Washington, D.C.: National Geographic Video, 2003).

## INTERNET SITES

Visit our Web page for lots of links about Benjamin Harrison and other U.S. presidents:

*http://www.childsworld.com/links*

*Note to Parents, Teachers, and Librarians:* We routinely verify our Web links to make sure they are safe, active sites—so encourage your readers to check them out!